What YOU Can Do to STOP BULLYING

Addy Ferguson

PowerKiDS press.

New York

Published in 2013 by The Rosen Publishing Group, Inc.
29 East 21st Street, New York, NY 10010

First Edition

Editor: Jennifer Way
Book Design: Erica Clendening and Colleen Bialecki

Photo Credits: Cover © iStockphoto/Daniel Laflor; p. 4 © iStockphoto/Adam Kazmierski; p. 5 Helder Almeida/Shutterstock.com; p. 6 © iStockphoto/Juanmonino; pp. 7, 9, 13 O Driscoll Imaging/Shutterstock.com; p. 10 © iStockphoto/AlbanyPictures; p. 11 Chris Clinton/Taxi/Getty Images; p. 12 Uniquely India/Getty Images; p. 14 Andersen Ross/The Image Bank/Getty Images; p. 15 Baerbel Schmidt/Stone/Getty Images; p. 17 © iStockphoto/Kristian Sekulic; p. 18 Digital Vision/Getty Images; p. 19 Robert E. Daemmrich/Stone/Getty Images; p. 20 PhotoLink/Photodisc/Getty Images; p. 21 © iStockphoto/Catherine Yeulet; p. 22 Jim Esposito/Blend Images/Getty Images.

Library of Congress Cataloging-in-Publication Data
Ferguson, Addy.
 What you can do to stop bullying / by Addy Ferguson. — 1st ed.
    p. cm. — (Stand up: bullying prevention)
 Includes index.
 ISBN 978-1-4488-9667-7 (library binding) — ISBN 978-1-4488-9792-6 (pbk.) —
 ISBN 978-1-4488-9793-3 (6-pack)
 1. Bullying—Prevention—Juvenile literature. 2. Aggressiveness in children—Juvenile literature. I. Title.
 BF637.B85F473 2013
 302.34'3—dc23
                                2012024146

Manufactured in the United States of America

CPSIA Compliance Information: Batch #W13PK4: For Further Information contact Rosen Publishing, New York, New York at 1-800-237-9932

Contents

What Is Bullying?

Do you know the difference between teasing and bullying? Teasing is generally good-natured and stops if the person being teased gets upset. Bullying is different. The bully is not trying to have fun. He is trying to hurt or scare the other person. Bullying does not stop when someone gets upset. It keeps happening or even gets worse.

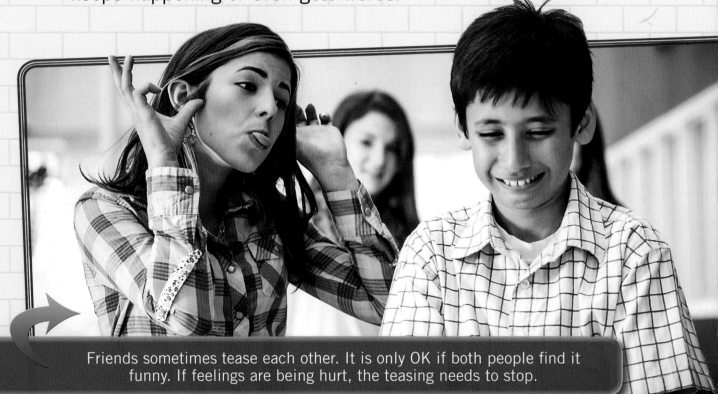

Friends sometimes tease each other. It is only OK if both people find it funny. If feelings are being hurt, the teasing needs to stop.

People who are being bullied might feel like no one cares about their problems.

You have likely seen someone get bullied at school. You may have wanted to help the person being bullied but were unsure what to do. This book will give you some ideas that will help you take action to stop bullying at your school.

More than One Kind of Bully

There are a few different kinds of bullies. **Verbal** bullies use words to hurt others. They may call their **victims** names, tell lies about them, or say mean things. **Physical** bullies push, shove, punch, or use other physical ways to hurt someone.

If you receive a text message from a cyberbully, do not respond to it. You should save the message to show to an adult, though.

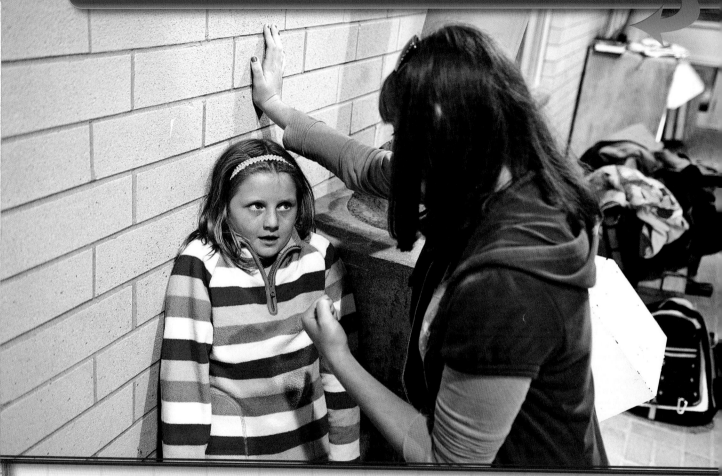

Some bullies will convince other people to ignore or **exclude** the victim. This is called relational bullying. There is also something called cyberbullying, which is bullying that happens over the Internet, through text messages, or via e-mail. No matter what kind of bullying it is, it is wrong. We each have the power to stop it, though.

Why Do People Bully?

Kids may start bullying others for different reasons. Some bullies are not treated well at home, either by parents or by brothers and sisters. Others bully because it gives them a feeling of control. It may help them feel better about their own angry feelings or **depression**.

Many people who are bullies do not feel **empathy** for others. They look down on other people and feel like they deserve to be bullied for acting or looking a certain way. These reasons are no excuse, though. There is never a good reason to bully another person.

Many bullies single out others to hurt because they think it makes them feel powerful.

Who Gets Bullied?

A bully may pick a victim based on how that person looks or acts. Bullies often choose shy or quiet kids to pick on. Sometimes a bully may target a kid who spends a lot of time alone.

Bullies often target kids who are loners because they do not have many friends who will stand up for them.

Being clumsy or bad at sports is another reason that kids might be bullied. This is why many kids dislike gym class or are afraid of using the school's locker rooms.

Students who other kids think are different can become targets for bullies, too. They could be people who look or dress differently or who behave in a way that others find annoying or odd. Sometimes, though, it is as simple as just being in the wrong place at the wrong time when a bully is looking for someone to pick on. Anyone can get bullied.

The Effects of Bullying

Think about how you would feel if someone said mean, hurtful, or **threatening** things to you. The victims of bullies likely feel that way every day. They may withdraw from activities and friends. They may seem sad, lonely, or worried. As they spend most of their time thinking about the bully, their grades suffer. All of these things can affect that person's life long after the bullying stops.

A kid who is being bullied may dread going to school. She might pretend she is sick so she can avoid bullying.

If you have a friend who is being bullied, he might withdraw because he is sad, embarrassed, or afraid you will be bullied for being his friend. Reach out to your friend!

Next time you see someone being bullied, think about how you would feel if you were in her place. You would want someone to step in and help you, right? There are things you can do to help!

Speak Up!

Did you know there is a name for the people who see bullying happen? These people are called **bystanders**. Bystanders may seem like they have nothing to do with the **conflict**. By staying quiet and not getting involved, though, they silently say that the bullying is okay with them.

You could talk to your parents about bullying. They may have advice about how you can speak up safely at school.

Speaking up when kids are bullying others can help change how bullying is dealt with at school.

You might be afraid that if you speak up, the bully will start picking on you. You might feel like whatever you do will not help. Do not feel this way. Speaking up is the right thing to do. You will feel better if you say something.

Buddy Up

You do not have to take on the school bully by yourself, though. Talk to your friends. If you agree to stand up to the bully together, it will feel easier to say something. It will also be harder for the bully to target you instead. Students who have been bystanders in the past might find the courage to stand up as well. Sometimes it just takes one person to start big changes.

You can also try to make friends with the bullied person. This will help that person see that she is not alone.

The buddy system is a good way to stand up to bullying. When you support each other, you will have more courage to tell bullies that what they are doing is wrong.

Talk to an Adult

Sometimes you might not feel safe speaking up on your own or with friends. Talk to a trusted adult and ask her to help you. A parent or teacher can come up with a plan to help the victim. She can think of a way to help the bully change, too.

A parent or other trusted adult could give you advice about dealing with bullying. She likely dealt with bullying as a kid and knows what you are going through.

Parents and teachers can work with a bullied kid to end the bullying. They can also help her deal with the effects of bullying.

If you tell a grown-up what is happening and she does not seem willing to help, do not give up. Find another adult who is willing to listen and find a solution. You might also talk with this person about putting an antibullying program in place.

Make Your School Bully Free

Some schools have decided to put antibullying **policies** in place. They may have met with students and agreed their school is a "bully-free zone." What does this mean?

Punishments like suspending a bully do not help him learn from what he did wrong. He also needs to learn how he can change his behavior.

If your school does not have a bullying policy, you could start a student group that works for those changes to be made.

Sometimes these policies use punishment to stop bullying. This does not work very well. It works better to get all the students to agree that bullying is not okay. They also must agree to include others. They need to use their voices when they see bullying happen. They all must also work together to make a safe place for everyone to go to school. Making a bully-free school is not easy, but it is worth it!

Respect for All

No one deserves to be bullied. All people deserve **respect**, even if they are not the same as we are or if we do not like them.

It is important to remember that the victim is not responsible for being bullied. He did not cause it or do anything that makes the bullying all right. Bullying is never all right. Do the right thing and speak up when a person is being hurt or bullied.

When everyone respects everyone else, school is a much happier place!

Glossary

bystanders (BY-stan-derz) People who are there while something is taking place but are not taking part in what is happening.

conflict (KON-flikt) A fight or a struggle.

depression (dih-PREH-shun) A sickness in which a person is very sad for a long time.

empathy (EM-puh-thee) Understanding and being aware of the feelings and thoughts of another person.

exclude (eks-KLOOD) To keep or shut someone out.

physical (FIH-zih-kul) Having to do with the body.

policies (PAH-luh-seez) Laws or rules that people use to help them make decisions.

respect (rih-SPEKT) Thinking highly of someone or something.

threatening (THREH-tun-ing) Acting as though something will possibly cause hurt.

verbal (VER-bul) Using words.

victims (VIK-timz) People or animals that are harmed or killed.

Index

B
bullies, 4, 6–8, 10–12, 15–16, 18
bystanders, 14, 16

D
depression, 8
difference, 4

E
e-mail, 7
empathy, 8

F
fun, 4

H
home, 8

I
Internet, 7

K
kid(s), 8, 10–11
kind(s), 6–7

P
parent(s), 8, 18
policies, 20–21
power, 7

S
school(s), 5, 20–21
sisters, 8

T
teasing, 4
text messages, 7

Websites

Due to the changing nature of Internet links, PowerKids Press has developed an online list of websites related to the subject of this book. This site is updated regularly. Please use this link to access the list:
www.powerkidslinks.com/subp/stop/